孝顺

Social Emotional and Multicultural Learning |
Non-Fiction Series

Copyright © 2022 by Level Learning, INC. and Washington Yu Ying PCS™
Original and Edited Text Copyright © 2022 by Washington Yu Ying PCS™

All rights reserved. No part of this book in whole or part may be reproduced without written permission from the publisher.

Published by Level Learning, INC.
Content Contributors:
Washington Yu Ying PCS™
Level Learning - Ya-Ching Chang

Illustrations by: Josh Taira

Leveling classification based on Level Learning standard. For full description, visit www.levellearning.com

ISBN 978-1-64040-091-7
Simplified Chinese Edition

About Level Learning:
Level Learning provides a literacy focused curriculum specifically designed for K-12 Chinese as a Second Language classrooms. Our program offers 20 levels of specific and detailed objectives, leveled texts and passages, mastery-based online assessment, and analytics to enable data-driven instruction. Level Learning reading curriculum for both literature and informational text emphasize grammar and comprehension skills to help teachers develop confident and independent Chinese language readers. The non-fiction series of books are specifically designed to support our informational text course based on multiple national standards. To learn more about our entire offering, visit www.levellearning.com.

About Washington Yu Ying PCS™:
Washington Yu Ying PCS is a Mandarin English dual language immersion International Baccalaureate (IB) World school. Yu Ying's mission is to inspire and prepare young people to create a better world by challenging them to reach their full potential in a nurturing Chinese/English educational environment. Yu Ying's comprehensive IB, dual immersion curriculum equips students with global competencies for success in the real world. As a leader in immersion education, Yu Ying is determined to advance Chinese language programs and global citizenry education by helping other schools create and strengthen their Chinese programs. For more information, email: products@washingtonyuying.org

孝顺是中国的传统美德。中国人认为在所有的美德中,孝顺应该排在第一位。懂得孝顺父母的人,一定有颗仁爱的心,也能用同样的爱对待身边的人和事物。

简单地说,孝顺就是顺从、尊敬和关心父母,在他们需要帮助或者年老的时候照顾他们。父母辛苦养育孩子成长,教导他们做人的道理,孩子也应该用爱来回报父母。

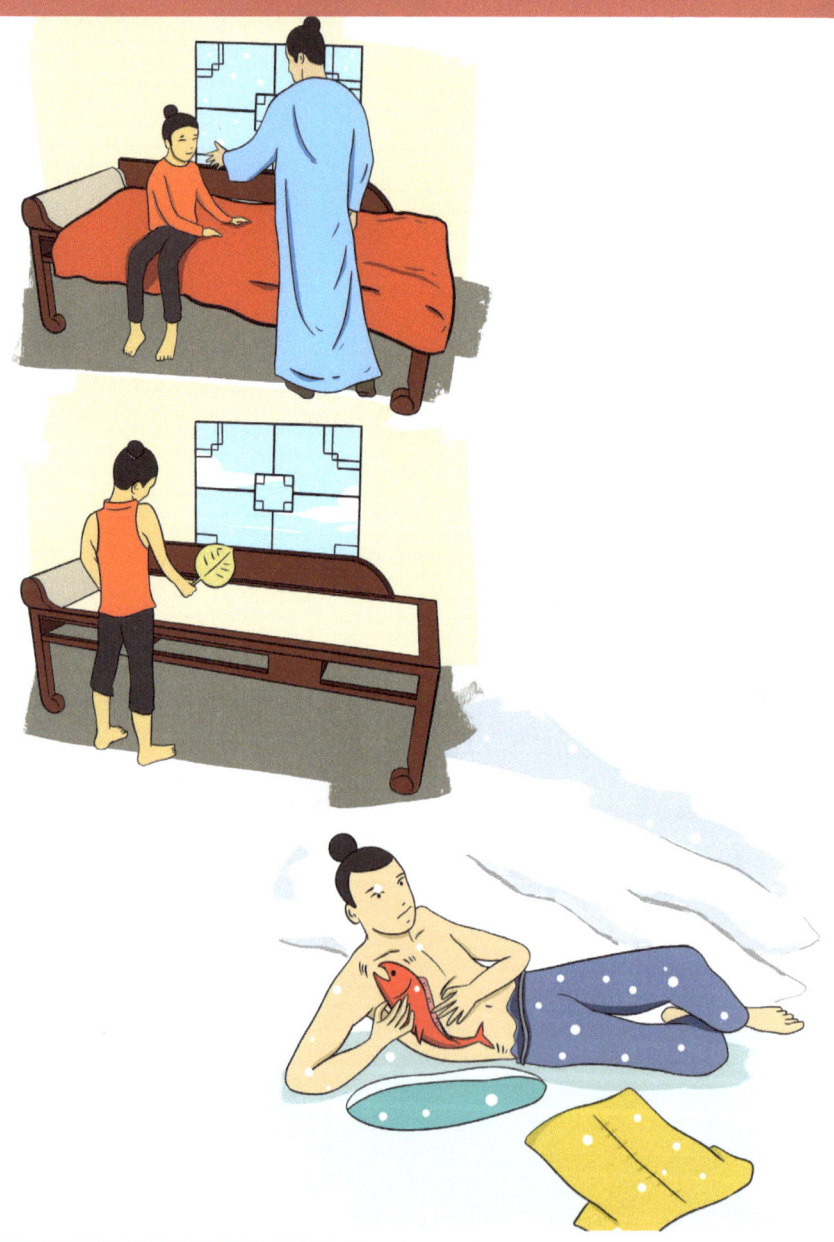

在中国历史上，有许多和孝顺有关的故事，其中最有名的就是"二十四孝"的故事。通过阅读这些故事，我们可以知道古时候的人是如何孝顺父母的。现在，我们就来读两个和孝顺有关的故事吧！

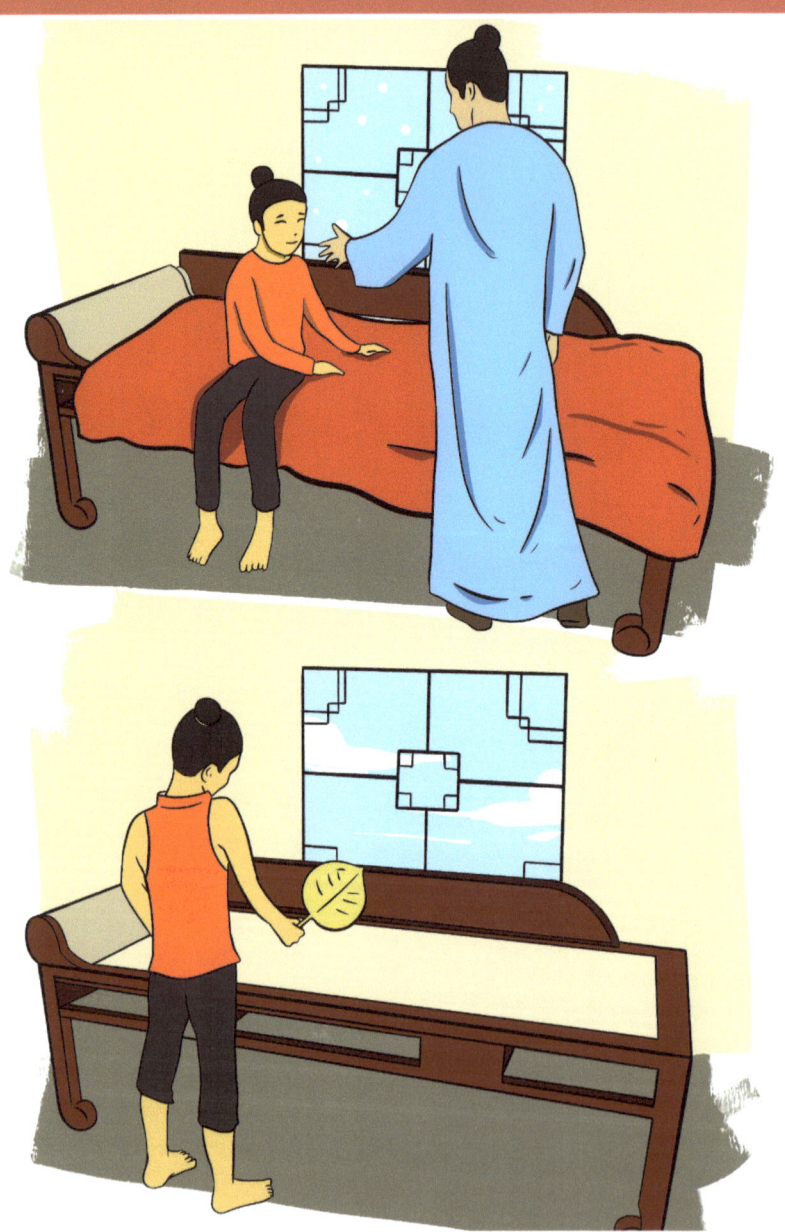

二十四孝里有个"黄香温席"的故事。这个故事是这样的：在寒冷的冬天，黄香担心父亲睡在冰冷的床上会生病。所以他总是先用自己的体温把棉被变暖和，再请父亲上床睡觉；如果是炎热的夏天，黄香就会先用扇子把父亲的床扇凉了，然后再请父亲上床睡觉。

另一个二十四孝的故事是"卧冰求鲤"，讲的是一个叫王祥的孝子，他的母亲想吃鱼，但是河水结冰，没办法捕捉鲤鱼。于是，王祥想到一个办法，他脱下衣服，躺在冰上，用体温溶化了寒冰，然后捉了好几条鲤鱼给母亲吃。

"黄香温席"和"卧冰求鲤"的故事都是中国古时候人们孝顺父母的好例子。直到今天，人们还在学习二十四孝的故事。学习这些故事不是鼓励人们按照里面的方法去做，而是让人们更懂得孝顺的重要。

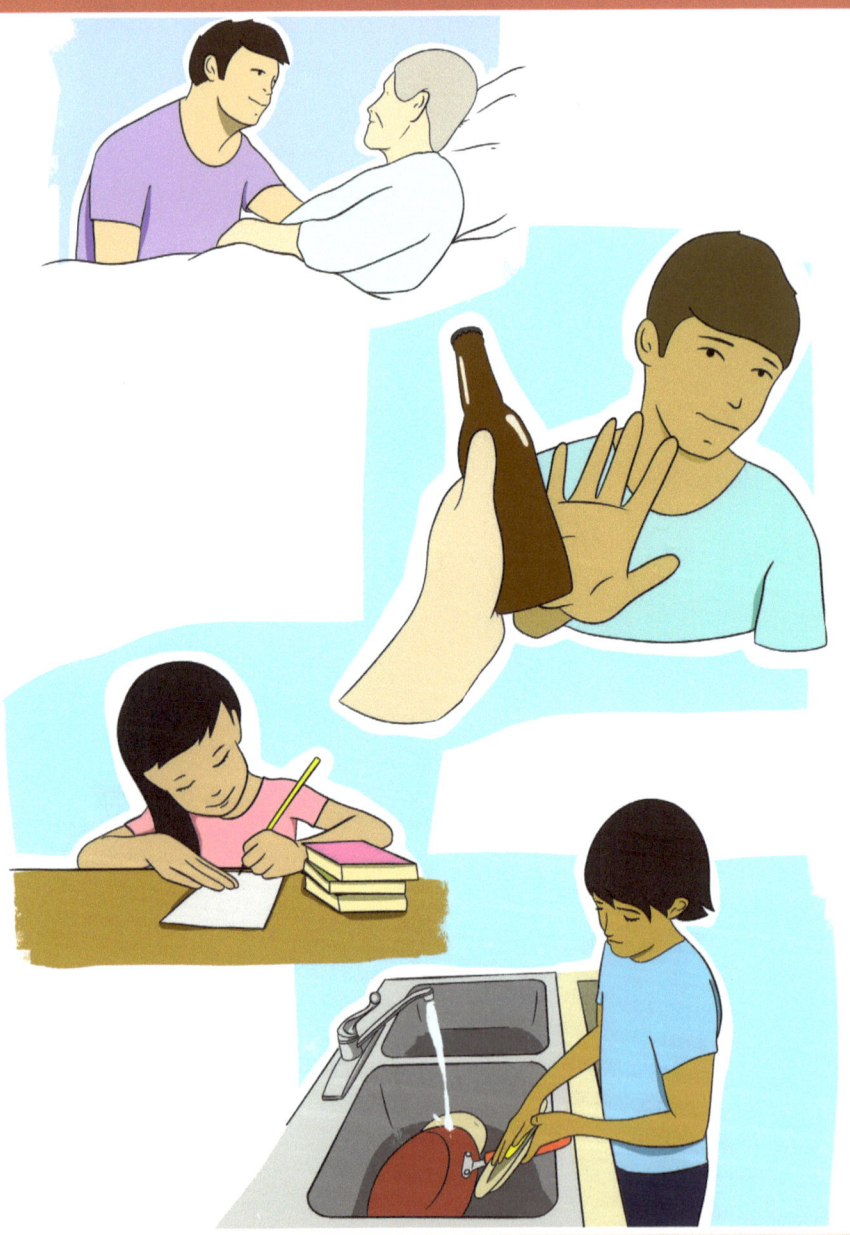

其实,孝顺父母有很多不同的方式。想想看,哪些是孝顺父母的表现呢?

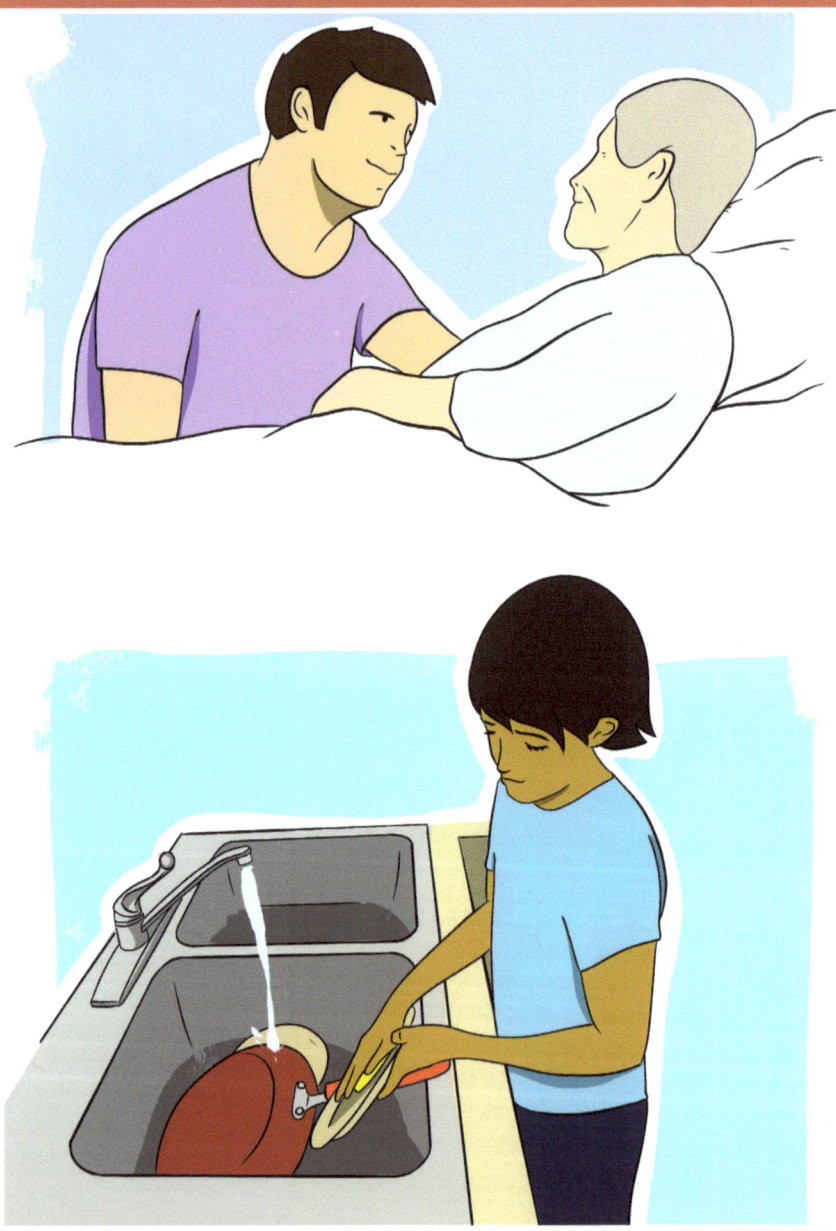

比如说，父母生病的时候，在身边照顾他们，这是一种孝顺的表现；就算不同意父母的观点，也不对父母大声说话或发脾气，这是一种孝顺的表现；体谅父母工作的辛苦，尽量帮他们分担家务，这也是一种孝顺的表现。

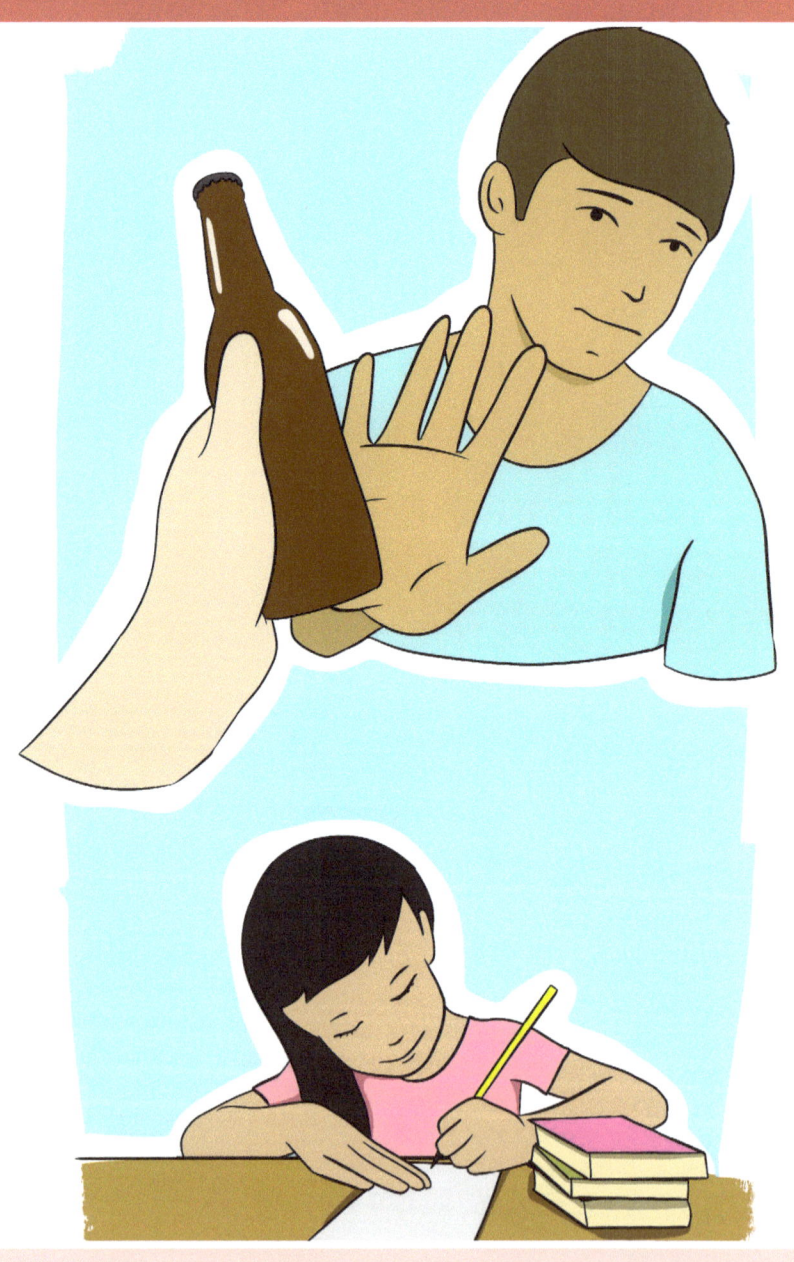

另外，不让父母为我们担心，也是一种孝顺。比如说，做好自己应该做的事情；为自己的学习负责；不让自己陷入危险；让父母知道自己的状况等。

其实，父母对孩子的爱是没有条件的，他们只希望孩子能够健康快乐地成长。写张卡片送给你的爸爸、妈妈，跟他们说一声："我爱你！"只要有心，时时刻刻想到父母，为他们带来快乐，这就是父母最想要的孝顺。

Glossary

	Pinyin	English Definition
孝顺	xiào shùn	filial piety, honor your parents
中国	zhōng guó	China
传统	chuán tǒng	tradition
美德	měi dé	virtue
认为	rèn wéi	to believe
位	wèi	position
懂	dǒng	understand
仁爱	rén ài	compassion, benevolent
对待	duì dài	to treat
身边	shēn biān	around
顺从	shùn cóng	obedient
尊敬	zūn jìng	to respect
关心	guān xīn	to care about
辛苦	xīn kǔ	exhausting
养育	yǎng yù	to rear, to bring up

	Pinyin	English Definition
成长	chéng zhǎng	growing up
教导	jiào dǎo	to teach
道理	dào lǐ	reason
回报	huí bào	to reciprocate, in return
历史	lìs hǐ	history
有关	yǒu guān	related
古时候	gǔ shí hou	in olden days
寒冷	hán lěng	cold
担心	dān xīn	to worry
冰冷	bīng lěng	ice-cold
体温	tǐ wēn	body temperature
棉被	mián bèi	quilt, comforter
暖和	nuǎn huo	warm
炎热	yán rè	hot
扇子	shàn zi	fan

Glossary

	Pinyin	English Definition
扇凉	shān liáng	use fan to cool
结冰	jié bīng	freeze
办法	bàn fǎ	method
捕捉	bǔ zhuō	to catch
鲤鱼	lǐ yú	carp (a kind of fish)
脱	tuō	to take off
躺	tǎng	to lie down
溶化	róng huà	melt
例子	lì zi	example
鼓励	gǔ lì	to encourage
按照	àn zhào	according to
照顾	zhào gù	to take care of
观点	guān diǎn	view
发脾气	fā pí qi	to get angry
尽量	jǐn liàng	as much as possible

	Pinyin	English Definition
分担	fēn dān	to share
家务	jiā wù	housework
陷入	xiàn rù	to get caught in
危险	wēi xiǎn	danger
状况	zhuàng kuàng	situation

www.ingramcontent.com/pod-product-compliance
Lightning Source LLC
Chambersburg PA
CBHW041221070526
44584CB00001B/36